Zwort's Nature Report: Forest Trail

Story by Paul Pitts
Illustrated by James Needham

While Zwort's transport sphere sped over the unexplored planet, he searched the forest below. "There are plenty of animals down there, but where are all the Earthlings?" he wondered.

With a beep the green Speaker Beeper light began blinking. "At last!" He landed just as a boy darted back into the thick pine trees from the clearing. Zwort jumped from the sphere and ran toward him.

"Please don't be frightened," he said. "I'm Zwort."

"My name is Brock," the boy spoke quietly, "and I don't really know why I'm here. But I had a strange feeling I should come to the clearing today."

"It worked!" Zwort clapped his hands. "I sent a signal for help and you answered it."

"Are you in trouble?" Brock asked.

Zwort laughed. "Not exactly, but I need to find someone who knows about this planet Earth. Someone who cares about it and the animals who live here."

The boy smiled. "Oh, it's my mother you want, she's a forest ranger. She'd be perfect for the job."

"Well, I was thinking about someone a little younger, someone a little shorter, someone like you!" Zwort handed him a sheet of paper. "Here are my instructions."

GALAXY TODAY
ARTICLE ASSIGNMENT: PROJECT F.A.R.

1. **F**IND ANIMALS ON THE PLANET EARTH.
2. **A**NALYZE EACH ONE FOR UNIQUE FEATURES.
3. **R**ECORD WHAT YOU LEARN FOR OUR READERS.

Dear Parent:

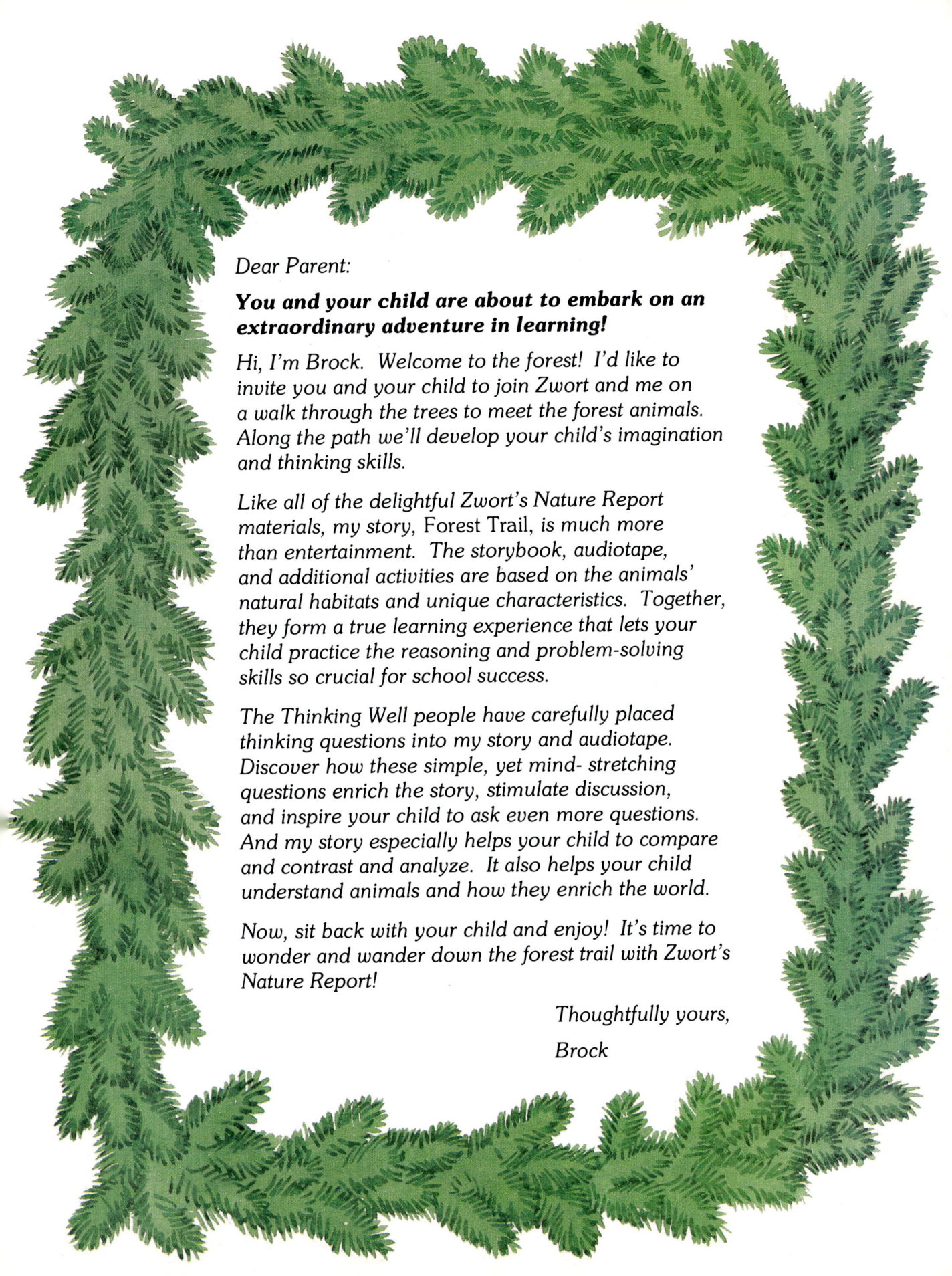

You and your child are about to embark on an extraordinary adventure in learning!

Hi, I'm Brock. Welcome to the forest! I'd like to invite you and your child to join Zwort and me on a walk through the trees to meet the forest animals. Along the path we'll develop your child's imagination and thinking skills.

Like all of the delightful Zwort's Nature Report materials, my story, Forest Trail, is much more than entertainment. The storybook, audiotape, and additional activities are based on the animals' natural habitats and unique characteristics. Together, they form a true learning experience that lets your child practice the reasoning and problem-solving skills so crucial for school success.

The Thinking Well people have carefully placed thinking questions into my story and audiotape. Discover how these simple, yet mind-stretching questions enrich the story, stimulate discussion, and inspire your child to ask even more questions. And my story especially helps your child to compare and contrast and analyze. It also helps your child understand animals and how they enrich the world.

Now, sit back with your child and enjoy! It's time to wonder and wander down the forest trail with Zwort's Nature Report!

Thoughtfully yours,

Brock

Copyright © 1991 Thinking Well

All rights reserved, including the right to reproduce this work or portions thereof in any form.

ISBN 1-55999-152-6

Thinking Well

A division of LinguiSystems, Inc.

Other products in the Zwort's Nature Report series:

Ocean Dive	*D102*
Safari Adventure	*D103*
Think 'n' Do Book: Forest, Ocean, Safari	*D104*
Animal Adventure: A Think 'n' Play Game	*D105*

Thinking Well
3100 4th Avenue
East Moline, IL 61244

1-800-U-2-THINK

Why did Brock think Zwort might be in trouble?
Why do you think Zwort wants a young person to help him?

"What's *Galaxy Today*?" Brock asked.

"That's a newspaper back home. As an intergalactic reporter, I'm doing an exclusive story about life on your planet, and I'm here to find out about forest animals," Zwort explained. "Will you help me, Brock?"

Brock looked at the paper again. "I might be able to help. My mother and I have spent lots of time here in the forest."

"You're perfect! I'm so glad to have found an Earthling child like you, and I know we'll be a great team." Zwort added, "I programmed my Speaker Beeper to find you, and it never makes a mistake."

"Speaker Beeper? What's a Speaker Beeper? How does it work?" Brock wondered.

"For one thing, it gives me directions to locate animals. Secondly, it acts as a recorder. And watch this." Zwort pointed his machine at a chattering squirrel. As the squirrel's noise reached the machine, it changed the sound into words.

"Hey, you two!" the squirrel was saying. "If you don't mind, this is *my* clearing and you have no business intruding here. Even if you do mind, hit the road!"

"That's amazing!" Brock gasped.

"You haven't seen anything yet, my Earthling friend. Let's go talk to some more animals!" Zwort headed across the clearing to a small stream with Brock right behind him.

Why do you think the squirrel is annoyed?

Zwort and Brock followed the stream until they came to a small animal groping in the ice cold water.

As the raccoon looked up, Zwort jumped. "Whoa, Brock, call the space police! I know all about Earthlings who wear masks. Come on, Brock, don't just stand there!"

"Chill out, man," said the animal. "Your data is defective."

"He's right, Zwort," Brock grinned. "This is a raccoon and the mask makes him handsome."

"Oops! I'm sorry. I'm new here," Zwort mumbled.

"Everything's cool," the raccoon said. "Especially this water, but it's dinnertime and . . . here comes the main course!"

"Gotcha!" A crayfish squirmed in his paw.

"Wow! What a catch!" Brock exclaimed.

"Am I cool or what? These long, strong fingers on my paws are flexible to the max. Watch!" The raccoon reached over and untied Brock's sneaker.

"Why, they should be called **hands**, not **paws**," Zwort said into the Speaker Beeper.

Zwort thinks the raccoon's paws should be called "hands." Do you agree? Why?

"Hey man, I'm sorry about how I look. I'm molting, like losing my winter fur. I do it every spring." The raccoon smoothed his paws over his fur.

"Does it hurt?" asked Zwort, rubbing his own smooth skin.

"No, man. With summer coming, I'm glad to have it happen," the raccoon responded cheerfully. "Actually, I have two kinds of hair, short, fine underfur for warmth and an overcoat of coarse guard hairs for protection. I lose a whole mountain of both kinds from early spring to summer."

"On my planet, we lost our hair millions of years ago," Zwort explained.

The raccoon told Zwort, "You've got to be patient, man. I just hang loose and slowly it grows back. My fur's thicker than ever by late fall."

"Our hair never grew back," Zwort said wistfully. He thought of all the readers of *Galaxy Today* who would be thrilled with just a handful of that mountain of hair.

"I'd suggest a raccoon cap," the animal said, "but that would put all my cousins in danger from hunters. Definitely not a smooth move!

"Speaking of hunting, man, I'd better get busy fishing for some more dinner."

"Happy fishing!" called Zwort and Brock.

Why would the raccoon's coat start getting longer and thicker in the fall?

A sharp rat-a-tat-tat above them caught Brock's attention. Grabbing Zwort's hand, Brock circled the dead pine tree a few feet away.

"Good grief, visitors!" said a woodpecker up above in the tree. He disappeared around the trunk. Zwort and Brock followed.

"Oh, no!" He flicked his wings, ready to take off.

"Wait! We just want to talk for a minute," called Brock.

"Talk?" The woodpecker's eyes darted nervously as he continued around the tree. "Talk about what?"

"You're a wonderful climber," said Zwort. The woodpecker stopped. "I'm sure your sharp claws help, but how come you don't slide backwards off the tree trunk?"

"It's simple really . . . my toes. Most birds have three in front and one in back. I have two in front and two in back. That gives me extra support," the woodpecker explained. "Then, I just brace my stiff tail feathers against the tree like so, and I'm secure! Now, if you'll excuse me . . ."

Why doesn't the woodpecker want to talk to Brock and Zwort?

The woodpecker's chisel-like beak clattered against the tree.

"Doesn't that give you a headache?" Brock covered his ears. "I'm getting one from just listening to that racket."

The woodpecker stopped. "Headache? Not at all. The strong muscles in my neck that make me such a speedy driller are great shock absorbers."

He glanced around quickly. "After I drill down to my insect lunch, my sticky tongue goes into action."

"My goodness, it's so long!" Zwort said.

Then, Zwort asked, "I know you have to eat, but doesn't your drilling damage the tree?"

"Now, wait a minute," the woodpecker flicked his wings. "Woodpeckers don't kill trees. No sir! We drill, looking for insects, insects that have already injured the tree."

His noisy battering started again like a small feathered jackhammer.

Do you think the woodpecker helps or hurts nature? Why?

"Who in the world is making all that racket? Can't a fella get some sleep? I've got a mighty big night coming up!"

"Sorry, we didn't mean to disturb your nap," said Brock.

"Who are you?" The porcupine squinted up at them. "My eyesight's never been all that good. What can I do for you?"

Zwort walked closer. "We're learning about forest animals."

"Well, what do you want to know, youngsters? *I'm* a forest animal," he said.

"A big one," observed Brock.

"That's 'cause I'm old. We porcupines keep growing as long as we live."

"Folks accuse me of being a mite slow," the porcupine yawned, "but why hurry if you don't have to?"

"How do you catch your food?" asked Zwort, thinking of the speedy raccoon.

The porcupine chuckled. "Trees don't run and that's what I eat – tree bark! This here forest is a real feast to me."

How is the forest like a feast to the porcupine?

"I never run, even when some rascal takes a notion to give me a bad time. I'm well equipped to deal with such foolishness. Take a look at this."

The porcupine's quills stuck straight out.

"Wow, you look like a mountain of little spears!" Brock stepped forward to take a closer look.

"If my attacker keeps coming closer, I get so dad-burned excited that I chatter and shake my tail back and forth. If that doesn't convince him," the porcupine added, "I'm afraid he's bound to leave with plenty of painful souvenirs in his skin."

"Yeowch! I can just imagine!" Zwort shivered, as Brock retreated behind him.

"Well, he can't say I didn't warn him!" the porcupine said.

He settled his quills back against his body. "Just thinking about all that excitement makes me tired. Please excuse me, young'uns. It's my naptime."

The porcupine started back toward the bush, then stopped and sniffed. "Phew!" He shuffled off in the opposite direction.

What do you think bothered the porcupine?

"Go ahead, run away. Everybody else does," said a skunk coming out of the bush. "Even my mate only stays around a day or two."

"We're not going anywhere," Zwort said firmly.

"You're not?" asked the skunk.

"My mother says that all animals are beautiful," Brock added. "Every animal has its own special beauty, and each one has its own place in nature's plan."

"Your mother is a smart person, Brock. I'm a very helpful animal," the skunk agreed.

"How do you help?" asked Zwort.

"Well," the skunk explained, "I eat a great variety of things, from insects to rodents, from fruit to garbage. My appetite removes an amazing number of pests from this world."

What are some of the animal pests the skunk might eat?

The skunk continued, "I'm not very big, I don't run very fast, I can't climb trees, and I hardly ever bite. I guess I'm lucky to produce a liquid with one of the strongest odors in the world."

Zwort picked up the skunk.

"Careful," said the animal. "The glands that hold my scent are right under my tail."

"I'll be careful." Zwort scratched her under the chin.

"If anyone bothers me, I stamp my feet and growl. If they don't leave, I turn my back, lift my tail, and spray! I can't help myself, it's an instinct!"

A loud snapping and cracking of underbrush came from the forest.

"I'd better be on my way," said the skunk, "or I might just have to use my aromatic weapon. I'd hate to leave you with that reminder of our visit. The smell lasts for days, you know!"

The skunk scurried back into the bushes.

Why do you think the skunk's smell lasts for days?

"Hello, sports fans!" said a head breaking through the underbrush. "A woodpecker told me you were in the area trying to find out about special animals, and I knew you'd want to talk to me."

"My goodness, you startled me," stammered Zwort.

"I am a little overwhelming," the moose said. "Actually, I think a better word for me is *impressive*."

Brock grinned. "Well, the word for you sure isn't *modest*!"

"I'm a natural athlete, you see." The moose tipped his head and nudged Brock with his antler. "For one thing, I'm one of the best runners in the world."

Zwort looked closely at the moose. "I think you've been doing too much running. Your hooves are falling apart!"

The moose snorted. "These are my special split hooves. They're broader and more flexible than a horse's hooves. That's why I can travel so fast through mossy, muddy marshland in the summer and deep snow in the winter."

He scraped his antlers against a tree.

"Nice horns," Brock said.

"You noticed! Six feet across, they're like a championship crown. I shed my horns every year. Then, it takes me about four and a half months every year to grow these beauties, but it's worth it. They're great protection."

How are the moose's antlers good protection for him?

"Did I mention I swim almost as well as I run?" the moose asked.

"No, but I'm sure we're going to hear about it," said Brock.

"If you don't believe it, sport, just follow me around for a day. I can eat plants off the bottom of a lake in water twenty feet deep."

"That's amazing," said Zwort. "Do you always swim that deep?"

"No, my favorite picnic spot is at the edge of a pond or stream with my head underwater just up to my ears. I graze till my mouth's full. Then I raise my head to chew so I can keep a lookout."

"I hate to say it, Zwort, but he's impressive all right," Brock admitted.

"I'd better go," said the moose. "Speed, stamina, keeping on the move – that's what life's all about. Nice talking with you."

He trotted into the forest without waiting for a reply.

When the moose eats, he raises his head to chew. What do you think he's keeping a lookout for?

A crash from the forest brought Zwort and Brock running.

"Less than five minutes to gnaw down that tree," said the thick-furred, shiny animal. "I'd like to see my dad top that!"

"It sounds like there's some competition going on around here," said Zwort. "What's the prize?"

The young beaver looked over. "Oh, hi. It's not a real contest, but I'm going on two years old now and, for a beaver, that means it's time to move out."

"You're leaving home?" Brock asked.

"Not today, but it's comin'. My folks will be bootin' me out. Oh, they'll let me stick around for the winter, until the new kits come along. Then it's adios, amigo."

Zwort patted his back. "That's too bad."

"Not really. I only hung around to help with this year's kits anyway. I'm ready for a change of scenery."

"I can match my dad, tree for tree, right now." He smiled. "It's these front teeth. The orange front on my teeth is as hard as a rock, but the back is softer. The back wears away a bit every time I gnaw on something, keeping the front edge sharp."

Brock carefully felt a tooth's edge. "So the orange part never wears away?"

"It does a little," he answered. "I do a lot of tree cutting. Luckily, my front teeth keep growing throughout my life. The trick is to balance out the wearing away caused by gnawing with the new growth."

What would happen to the beaver's teeth if he stopped cutting down trees and rested for a couple of months?

"Yep, come spring, I'll hit the road. I'll find my own area to fix up . . . build a dam, lay in a supply of saplings, and start construction on my own lodge."

"It sounds exciting, but it must take a lot of work," Zwort said.

"My mother says that the beaver is like a doctor, healing the land," Brock explained. "He builds dams which make ponds of water. The ponds fill up with rich soil over the years, forming meadows. New plants grow and animals can find food and make homes."

"Not bad work for this Earth, is it?" said the beaver proudly. He began gnawing a branch from the fallen tree.

"Well, Brock, I think I have enough information to start my article," Zwort said, turning back the way they had come. "Like our beaver friend here, it's time for me to move on."

"So soon?" Brock asked.

"Your mom will be expecting you home." Zwort gave the boy a hug. "Thanks for coming along. I'm going to miss you."

"Me, too," said Brock. "I'll be waiting for our trails to cross again."

Think 'n' Tell

If the animals were people, which animal in this story would be a grandpa? Which animal would be a grandson?

Which animal's eating habits harm the trees? How does it happen?

The moose has no quills like a porcupine or spray like the skunk. How does a moose protect itself?

Which animal would you like to ask a question? What would you ask?

Several of the animals in this book are nocturnal, or hunt at night. They use the dark as an extra type of protection. Which animals do you think might be nocturnal hunters? Why?

Moose's Antlers

Think 'n' Do

It takes four and a half months for a moose to grow his antlers each year. You can have a pair for yourself in much less time!

What you need: paper bag   pencil
                        scissors   ruler
                        stapler

What to do:

1. Cut a large paper bag open on the seam. Cut the bottom off the bag.

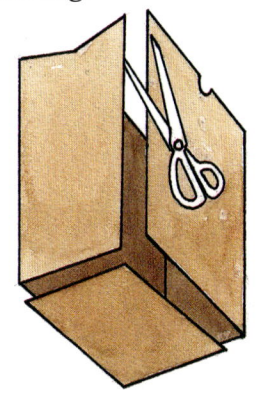

2. Fold the bag in half. Place the folded side on your left and draw a line across your paper, 2" from the bottom. This piece will be the headband of your antlers.

3. Draw another line 1" from the fold. Make your line like the example.

4. Place your left hand beneath your line so your fingertip extends an inch or two beyond the line. Trace around your hand. Extend the line from your thumb back to the headband.

5. Cut out your antlers while the bag is folded. Make sure you don't cut into the space for the headband.

6. Open up the paper. Try on the moose antlers for size. Then, have a parent staple the ends of the bag together so it fits your head like a headband.

The moose said his antlers provide good protection. When do you think the antlers might be a problem for the moose?

Does This Make Sense?

Think 'n' Do

The skunk expects everyone to turn away from him. Why do you think that is? Does a skunk smell all the time?

Sometimes our sense of sight makes us think we smell something, and our sense of smell can make a difference in what we taste. Try this simple experiment about your sense of smell and taste.

What you need:

apple   potato   carrot   pear   turnip   dishtowel

What to do:

1. Wash and peel the fruits and vegetables. Cut three or four pieces of each fruit into 1" squares.

2. Taste a piece of an apple and potato with your nose plugged. Do they taste different than they do when you can smell them?

3. Use the dishtowel for a blindfold. Then, blindfold a friend or have a friend blindfold you. Offer the blindfolded person one piece of the test food while he holds his nose. Can he recognize which food it is? Continue until the blindfolded person has tasted all the test foods.

4. Trade places so the other person can take the test.

Would you enjoy your food as much if you didn't have a sense of smell? Why? How does your sense of touch affect your sense of taste?

I'm Thinking Of . . .?

Think 'n' Do

Brock loves to play guessing games with his friends. You can play a guessing game with your forest friends cube!

What to do:

The first player, or the thinker, rolls the cube and looks at the animal that lands faceup. He thinks of something that animal can do. For example, if a raccoon lands faceup, the player might think that the raccoon is fast.

The other players, or questioners, have 5 chances to guess what the other player is thinking. If a questioner guesses right, he gets a point. If the guesses are all wrong, the thinker gets a point.

Then, the forest friend cube is passed to the next player and she becomes the thinker.

The first player who earns 4 points wins.

Is the thinker the only one thinking during this game? Why?

Zwort's Forest Song

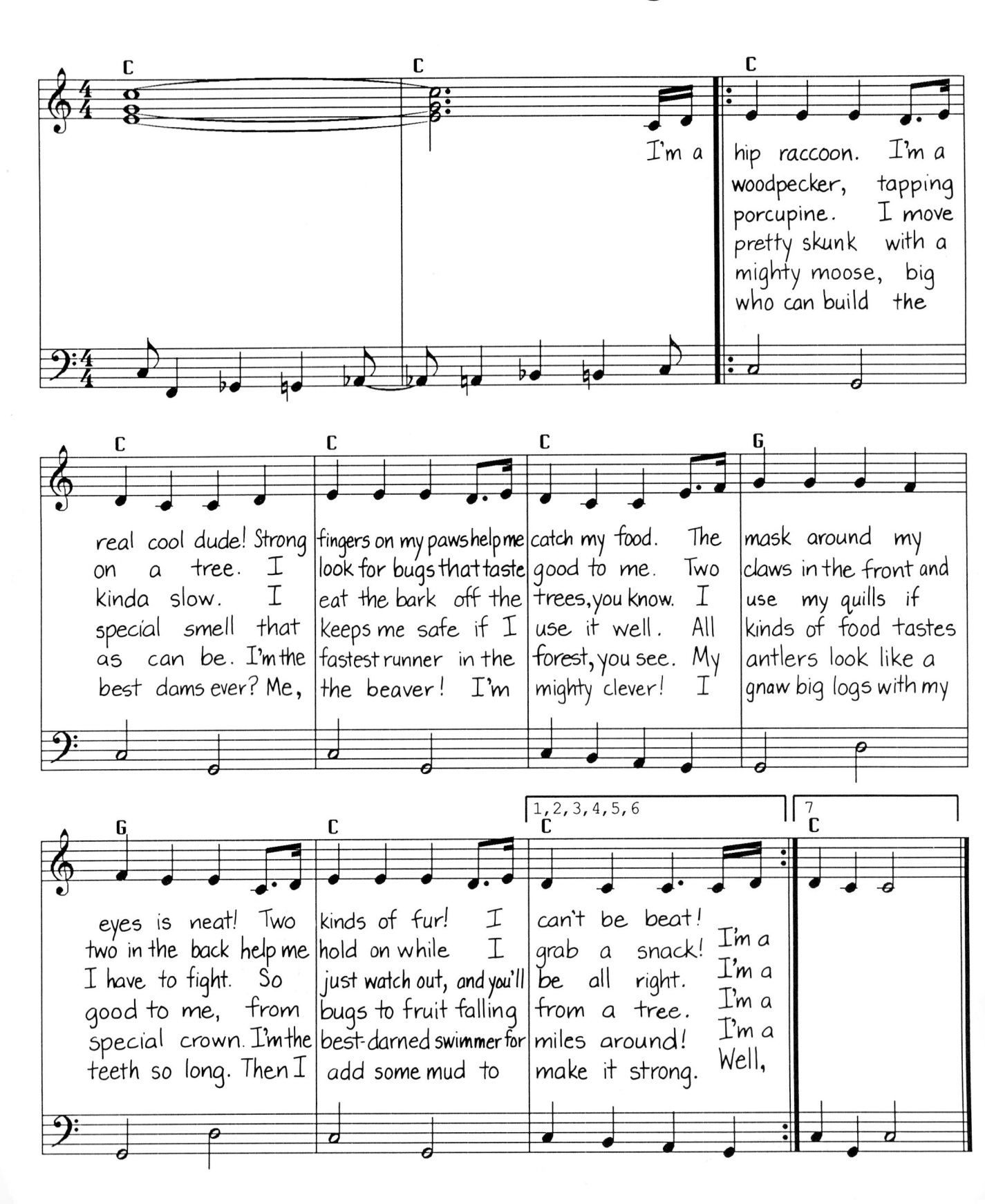

I'm a hip raccoon. I'm a woodpecker, tapping porcupine. I move pretty skunk with a mighty moose, big who can build the real cool dude! Strong fingers on my paws help me catch my food. The mask around my on a tree. I look for bugs that taste good to me. Two claws in the front and kinda slow. I eat the bark off the trees, you know. I use my quills if special smell that keeps me safe if I use it well. All kinds of food tastes as can be. I'm the fastest runner in the forest, you see. My antlers look like a best dams ever? Me, the beaver! I'm mighty clever! I gnaw big logs with my eyes is neat! Two kinds of fur! I can't be beat! I'm a two in the back help me hold on while I grab a snack! I'm a I have to fight. So just watch out, and you'll be all right. I'm a good to me, from bugs to fruit falling from a tree. I'm a special crown. I'm the best-darned swimmer for miles around! I'm a teeth so long. Then I add some mud to make it strong. Well,